MW00887743

Journal

Your

Journey

Discovery ~ Explant ~ Healing

© 2019 Tara Hopko

All rights reserved. No part of this publication may be printed, reproduced, stored in a retrieval system, or transmitted, emailed, uploaded in any form or by any means, electronic, mechanical, photocopying, recording, or otherwise, without the prior written permission of the publisher.

Published by T & MH Services

Printing in the United States of America
First printing 2019
IBN #9781711029122

♥ Journal Your Journey ♥

This journal is dedicated to all my Breast Implant Illness sisters who continue to help me heal. I would be lost without the love, support and guidance I receive from all of you. We are truly a community of warriors and knowing all of you has been the silver lining to the trauma of Breast Implant Illness.

So many amazing souls have opened their hearts to me after writing my story "Let Me Get This OFF My CHEST". Through these beautiful women and my own healing, I have learned that the journey of Breast Implant Illness is a long one, lasting way beyond discovery and explant. Healing from Breast Implant Illness may take years for most of us. Like any traumatic event in our lives, healing is a process. How we heal is a choice. I hope this journal will inspire you to heal in such a way, that after the dust has settled from BII, you find that you have become a 'better version of your old self'.

Breast Implant Illness is a road full of crazy, beautiful twists and turns. With each step of your journey, there will be beautiful blessings! If you don't take the time to honor the process, you may just miss life's gifts along the way.

This journal was designed for all my Breast Implant Illness sisters; those suffering with implants either from enhancement or reconstruction. It's for warriors waiting to explant or those who have just explanted. Make this a place to come and reflect throughout your experience. I have created this journal because I recognize that women who experience Breast Implant Illness all have one thing in common...

♥ Journal Your Journey ♥

we are never the same after this illness. It transforms and inspires us, if we allow it. Taking time to reflect on my own path to healing, I realized how remarkable it would have been to have documented my healing journey along the way.

Thank you for allowing me to guide you on your path to healing. When the road gets rough, remember, you are not alone. Times when you worry that your healing is not as much as the next girl, focus on the small successes. Be confident that explant is the only way to allow yourself to become happy and healthy again. Never forget that you are a warrior! Embrace your story and this storm through which you are walking.

As you Journal your Journey, allow these moments to transform you into the 'who' you are truly meant to be.

♥Tara

♥ Journal Your Journey ♥

Discovery

"I am not what happened to me,
I am what I choose to become."

~C.G. Jung

~Discovery~

You have just discovered Breast Implant Illness!

This is often a lot to process. While it's exciting to learn the cause of your illness, it's an overwhelming amount of information to absorb.

How did you discover that your implants are what has been making you so ill? Did you stumble upon it through social media? Did someone very courageously share their knowledge or their personal story with you? Was it was a medical professional that told you to look into your implants being the cause of your ailments?

_____

_____

_____

_____

_____

_____

_____

What are your initial feelings about what you've just learned? Did you experience a period of denial at first or were you confident that you are suffering from Breast Implant Illness?

_____

_____

_____

_____

_____

_____

_____

_____

_____

_____

_____

_____

_____

_____

_____

Symptoms

Mark off the current symptoms of Breast Implant Illness you are experiencing. This will be a great place to refer back to after explant when you begin to heal.

- ☐ Chronic Fatigue
- ☐ Ear Ringing
- ☐ Swollen Lymph Nodes
- ☐ Anxiety/Panic Attacks
- ☐ Brain Fog
- ☐ Skin Rashes
- ☐ Heart Palpitations
- ☐ Frequent Urination
- ☐ Night Sweats
- ☐ Sensitivity to Sound
- ☐ Difficulty Swallowing
- ☐ Low Libido
- ☐ Muscle Weakness
- ☐ Sensitivity to Light

- ☐ Fever
- ☐ Acne
- ☐ Vision Issues
- ☐ Hair Loss
- ☐ Depression
- ☐ Food Intolerances
- ☐ Insomnia
- ☐ Weight Gain/Loss
- ☐ Silent Reflux
- ☐ Joint Pain
- ☐ GI Issues
- ☐ Candida
- ☐ Migraines
- ☐ Dry Eyes

- [ ] Dehydration

- [ ] Intolerance to Heat or Cold

- [ ] Leaky Gut, IBS or SIBO

- [ ] Recurrent Infections

- [ ] Pain/Burning around Implants

- [ ] Hypo/Hyper Thyroid Symptoms

- [ ] Hypo/Hyper Adrenal Symptoms

- [ ] Symptoms of Fibromyalgia

- [ ] Symptoms of Lyme Disease

- [ ] Symptoms of EBV

- [ ] Mast Cell Activation Syndrome

- [ ] Feeling Like You Are Dying

- [ ] Symptoms/Diagnosis of Auto-Immune disease

    - [ ] Other _____

    - [ ] Other _____

    - [ ] Other _____

_____

_____

Symptoms list from <u>www.healingbreastimplantillness.com</u>

Now that you are aware that the symptoms you are experiencing have been caused by your implants, reflect back and think about when you first began to experience adverse effects. Looking back, what were the signs you missed?

_____

_____

_____

_____

_____

_____

_____

_____

_____

_____

_____

_____

_____

_____

_____

_____

Explant

"FAITH does not mean trusting God to stop the storm,

but trusting Him to strengthen us

as we walk through the storm."

~Unknown

Finding your Doctor

It is important to find a surgeon who is right for you. Although it would be nice, your surgeon does NOT have to believe in Breast Implant Illness. The surgeon you choose should be able to guarantee he/she will remove all of your capsule (scar tissue surrounding your implant).

SURGEONS TO CONSULT WITH

Dr. Name:

Phone #

Location:

Consult Fee:

Appointment Date/Time:

Notes:

SURGEONS TO CONSULT WITH

Dr. Name:

Phone #

Location:

Consult Fee:

Appointment Date/Time:

Notes:

Dr. Name:

Phone #

Location:

Consult Fee:

Appointment Date/Time:

Notes:

Consultations

Always be prepared at your consultations with a list of questions

to ask the surgeon.

(Full list of questions at www.healingbreastimplantillness.com)

Consultation #1

How many explants have you performed?

Where do you perform surgery?

Can you guarantee you will remove all capsule (scar-tissue) via

Total Capsulectomy or Enbloc?

How long will surgery take?

Are you willing to take photos/video of the surgery?

_____

_____

If I so desire, are you willing to return my implants to me?

_____

_____

Will I have drains?

_____

_____

_____

What pathology testing will be done?

_____

_____

_____

Do you recommend I need a lift?

_____

_____

_____

Approximately how long will my recovery be?

_____

_____

_____

_____

What testing needs to be done prior to surgery?

_____

_____

_____

_____

_____

Notes:

_____

_____

_____

_____

_____

_____

_____

_____

_____

_____

_____

Consultation #2

How many explants have you performed?

Where do you perform surgery?

Can you guarantee you will remove all capsule (scar-tissue) via
Total Capsulectomy or Enbloc?

How long will surgery take?

Are you willing to take photos/video of the surgery?

If I so desire, are you willing to return my implants to me?

Will I have drains?

What pathology testing will be done?

_____

_____

Do you recommend I need a lift?

_____

_____

_____

Approximately how long will my recovery be?

_____

_____

What testing needs to be done prior to surgery?

_____

_____

_____

Notes:

_____

_____

_____

_____

_____

Consultation #3

How many explants have you performed?

Where do you perform surgery?

Can you guarantee you will remove all capsule (scar -tissue) via
Total Capsulectomy or Enbloc?

How long will surgery take?

Are you willing to take photos/video of the surgery?

If I so desire, are you willing to return my implants to me?

Will I have drains?

What pathology testing will be done?

_____

_____

_____

Do you recommend I need a lift?

_____

_____

Approximately how long will my recovery be?

_____

_____

What testing needs to be done prior to surgery?

_____

_____

Notes:

_____

_____

_____

_____

_____

Physically Preparing

for Explant

What tests, if any, are needed prior to explant? Be sure to ask your surgeon what physicals/tests/imaging/lab work are required. (Note: Proceed with caution if a mammogram is requested as the integrity of your implants could already be compromised)

_____

_____

_____

_____

_____

_____

_____

_____

_____

_____

_____

Suggestions for Surgery

Helpful items to have as you recover...

- ☐ Small pillow (for in-between your chest & seatbelt)
- ☐ Arnica tablets   (for pain/bruising)
- ☐ Laxative   (Colace, Clearlax, Magnesium powder calm)
- ☐ A Recliner (It's more comfortable to sleep upright)
- ☐ Body Pillow and/or Extra Pillows to prop yourself up
- ☐ Front button/zip up top (w/inside pockets for drains if possible)
- ☐ Slip on shoes
- ☐ Dry shampoo (until you can wash your hair)
- ☐ Drawstring pants/leggings (because they are comfy)
- ☐ Tylenol (for when you decide to stop pain meds)
- ☐ Frozen veggies (great as ice packs if doctor approves)
- ☐ CBD oil
- ☐ Front closure bra (buy a few sizes & return unused)

♥ Journal Your Journey ♥

☐ Bendable straws (makes drinking easier if immobile)

☐ Neck pillow

☐ Healthy snacks (keep easily accessible for reaching)

☐ Easy meals (premade healthy meals)

☐ Baby wipes (to keep you clean & fresh until shower)

☐ Probiotics (to help your already compromised gut)

☐ Thermometer

☐ Throat lozenges

☐ Herbal hot pack (for shoulders & back-NOT breasts)

☐ Back scratcher

☐ Thin maxi-pads (for between your bra and scars)

☐ Before/After pics of your breasts & no filter face

_____

_____

_____

_____

_____

_____

Emotionally Preparing

...for Explant

There are a lot of emotions that come with deciding to explant. Many times, we are left feeling angry, scared, frustrated, uncertain that the implants are what is causing our symptoms, etc. Healing can begin before explant happens but you must honor the feelings that come. Keeping your mindset in a positive state will allow you to become emotionally ready for the journey you are about to embark on.

Many women find they are scared about not surviving long enough to have surgery, not waking up from surgery or scared about not healing.

What are you most frightened of?

_____

_____

_____

I found that talking with my pastor and the power of prayer helped me to overcome my fears before surgery. What are some ways you can overcome your fears?

Can any one of you by worrying add a single hour to your life
Matthew 6:27

_____

_____

_____

_____

_____

_____

_____

_____

_____

_____

_____

_____

_____

Have you spoken to your family/friends about your decision to explant?

If you have, how did it feel to tell them? Were you met with doubt and resistance or support & love?

If you have not yet told them, what is holding you back and how can you get through that?

_____

_____

_____

_____

_____

_____

_____

_____

_____

_____

_____

_____

Having support along this journey is a priceless gift! Who has given you the most support up to this point? Write a note of appreciation to this person so you can share it with them down the road.

Dear~

_____

_____

_____

_____

_____

_____

_____

_____

_____

_____

_____

_____

_____

_____

_____

A huge part of becoming emotionally prepared for explant is FORGIVENESS. Forgiving yourself for what you did not know in the past is key to healing. You must forgive yourself for the decisions that brought you to this point. Had you known better; you may have made different choices.

Forgive yourself. Not just once.
Again, and again, and again.
As many times as it takes to find peace.
~Unknown~

~Write a letter of FORGIVENESS to yourself~

Dear Me~

_____

_____

_____

_____

_____

_____

_____

_____

To mentally prepare for your explant journey, I find that it's helpful to begin visualizing what it will look and feel like to be healthy & whole again. Take some time to envision & document what your life will look & feel like after explant; to be living and loving life again!

_____

_____

_____

_____

_____

_____

_____

_____

_____

_____

_____

_____

_____

_____

_____

_____

Many women feel a great sense of regret or being misled in the decision of getting their implants. It's time to LET THAT GO... right here, right now. Use these lines to get out the anger you have toward what led you to the decision of getting your implants.

The anger that we hold is an extension of our implants, an emotional poison that will weigh you down. Let that go and be grateful. Grateful for your journey, your story, your body that fought like a warrior and won the war.
~Tara Hopko

Right here, right now ~ I am letting go of....

_____

_____

_____

_____

_____

_____

_____

_____

_____

~The Lighter Side~

Let's dedicate this space to how you are feeling the night before surgery. (Heck, you're probably not sleeping anyway ;-)

To fully commit to this process, we must get you to a place of peace & calm for your surgery. You've taken the time to fully prepare your mind and your body for this journey it's about to embark on.

Days, weeks, months & years ahead you will look back on this night with an overwhelming feeling of pride for how brave you were.

Tend to your soul now. You have fought through this storm for quite some time. You've been to countless doctors; you've listened to unsuccessful but well-intended advice, with no relief. The relief will be found in your explant surgery. It is at this very moment, when you take this leap of faith that you must truly believe your prayers have been answered and 'All will be well'.

♥ Journal Your Journey ♥

Then they cried out to the LORD in their trouble,
and he brought them out of their distress.
He stilled the storm to a whisper;
The waves of the sea were hushed.
They were glad when it grew calm,
and he guided them to their desired haven.
Psalm 107:28

_____

_____

_____

_____

_____

_____

_____

_____

_____

_____

_____

_____

_____

_____

_____

_____

~Surgery~

What were your first thoughts when you woke up from surgery? How did you feel immediately after, both physically and emotionally? How does it feel to have surgery behind you now?

_____

_____

_____

_____

_____

_____

_____

_____

_____

_____

_____

_____

_____

Freedom!!!

How does it feel to be free of your toxic implants?

What are some of the first changes you notice after explant?

_____

_____

_____

_____

_____

_____

_____

_____

_____

_____

_____

_____

_____

~First Look~

Let's be honest, many of us feel apprehensive about seeing our chest after surgery. Some women are left with very little breasts, some none at all and others are sometimes pleasantly surprised with their results.

As you take that first look, what are your thoughts? Remember that it's OK to not feel OK with how you look right away. Acceptance may take time.

"Being happy doesn't mean
that everything is perfect.
It means that you've decided to look
beyond the imperfections".
~Unknown~

_____
_____
_____
_____
_____
_____

~Recovery~

Recovering from surgery is the first step to healing. After explant, we are so anxious to begin healing that we forget to allow ourselves time to recover from surgery. Explant surgery is a major procedure! Immediately after, you must allow your body time to recover. Anesthesia alone takes weeks to detox from, especially for those of us who are positive for the MTHFR gene. So, after surgery, remind yourself that recovery is only the FIRST step to healing.

While recovering from surgery, support your system with healthy foods, lots of water and rest as much as you can! Don't put too much pressure on yourself to begin 'feeling the heal' right away. The heal will come but it will come in YOUR own time.

Listen... if your body could talk, she'd say... "I've been through a lot, I've fought for you for years while you had implants and I kept you well for as long as I could. Now that you've helped me by explanting, I am working hard to detox us from all the toxins and chemicals. Please be kind to me, talk to me with a loving spirit, I need to be praised, cherished and thanked now and again for all that I do!"

After you have recovered from surgery and the heal begins to happen, as do the flares... remind yourself now and again how far you've come. Remember how long you were sick. Remember just how sick you were. Some women wake from surgery feeling immediate relief, for others relief comes a bit later. Take these things into consideration when silently comparing your recovery and heal to the next girl. Take photos so you can see for yourself how the heal is happening! Every small improvement is a step toward healing, so be sure to take notice of subtle changes. Listen to your body, honor what she needs. Support her while she continues to fight like a warrior!

YOU ARE STRONGER THAN YOU KNOW!

Everyone's recovery looks different. No recovery is wrong. Take some time to note how your recovery looks. This will help down the road when you want to recall how far you've come.

   ~ How is your pain?
   ~ How are you able to manage your pain?
   ~ How long did you have drains in?
   ~ How did you sleep?

_____

_____

_____

_____

_____

_____

_____

_____

_____

_____

_____

Physical Healing

Refer back to this portion of the journal often.

Use this section as a place to document

your physical healing journey.

~Changes~

No matter how big or small, changes are happening!

Use this space to come back and document the positive changes

that are happening physically since your explant.

Week 1 post op
_____
_____
_____
_____
_____
_____

Week 2 post op
_____
_____
_____
_____
_____
_____

Week 3 post op

1 month post op

Symptoms ~ 1 month

At your one-month mark, take note as to what symptoms have disappeared and what still remains?

☐ Chronic Fatigue   ☐ Fever

☐ Ear Ringing   ☐ Acne

☐ Swollen Lymph Nodes   ☐ Vision Issues

☐ Anxiety/Panic Attacks   ☐ Hair Loss

☐ Brain Fog   ☐ Depression

☐ Skin Rashes   ☐ Food Intolerances

☐ Heart Palpitations   ☐ Insomnia

☐ Frequent Urination   ☐ Weight Gain/Loss

☐ Night Sweats   ☐ Silent Reflux

☐ Sensitivity to Sound   ☐ Joint Pain

☐ Difficulty Swallowing   ☐ GI Issues

☐ Low Libido   ☐ Candida

☐ Muscle Weakness   ☐ Migraines

☐ Sensitivity to Light   ☐ Dry Eyes

☐ Dehydration

☐ Intolerance to Heat or Cold

☐ Leaky Gut, IBS or SIBO

☐ Recurrent Infections

☐ Pain/Burning around Implants

☐ Hypo/Hyper Thyroid Symptoms

☐ Hypo/Hyper Adrenal Symptoms

☐ Symptoms of Fibromyalgia

☐ Symptoms of Lyme Disease

☐ Symptoms of EBV

☐ Mast Cell Activation Syndrome

☐ Feeling Like You Are Dying

☐ Symptoms/Diagnosis of Auto-Immune disease

    ☐ Other _____

    ☐ Other _____

    ☐ Other _____

Symptoms list from www.healingbreastimplantillness.com

♥ Journal Your Journey ♥

2 months post op

_____

_____

_____

_____

_____

_____

_____

_____

_____

3 months post op

_____

_____

_____

_____

_____

_____

_____

_____

Symptoms~ 3 months

At three months post op, what symptoms are still lingering? Looking back to the beginning of your journal, I bet there are many symptoms you have been able to say good-bye to!

☐ Chronic Fatigue   ☐ Fever

☐ Ear Ringing   ☐ Acne

☐ Swollen Lymph Nodes   ☐ Vision Issues

☐ Anxiety/Panic Attacks   ☐ Hair Loss

☐ Brain Fog   ☐ Depression

☐ Skin Rashes   ☐ Food Intolerances

☐ Heart Palpitations   ☐ Insomnia

☐ Frequent Urination   ☐ Weight Gain/Loss

☐ Night Sweats   ☐ Silent Reflux

☐ Sensitivity to Sound   ☐ Joint Pain

☐ Difficulty Swallowing   ☐ GI Issues

☐ Low Libido   ☐ Candida

☐ Muscle Weakness   ☐ Migraines

☐ Sensitivity to Light   ☐ Dry Eyes

☐ Dehydration

☐ Intolerance to Heat or Cold

☐ Leaky Gut, IBS or SIBO

☐ Recurrent Infections

☐ Pain/Burning around Implants

☐ Hypo/Hyper Thyroid Symptoms

☐ Hypo/Hyper Adrenal Symptoms

☐ Symptoms of Fibromyalgia

☐ Symptoms of Lyme Disease

☐ Symptoms of EBV

☐ Mast Cell Activation Syndrome

☐ Feeling Like You Are Dying

☐ Symptoms/Diagnosis of Auto-Immune disease

    ☐ Other _____

    ☐ Other _____

    ☐ Other _____

_____

_____

_____

Symptoms list from <u>www.healingbreastimplantillness.com</u>

6 months post op

_____
_____
_____
_____
_____
_____
_____
_____

9 months post op

_____
_____
_____
_____
_____
_____
_____
_____
_____
_____

1 year post op ~ Happy Explantiversary

♥ Journal Your Journey ♥

Symptoms~ 1 year

What are the few BII symptoms you are left with at your one year explantiversary?

☐ Chronic Fatigue   ☐ Fever

☐ Ear Ringing   ☐ Acne

☐ Swollen Lymph Nodes   ☐ Vision Issues

☐ Anxiety/Panic Attacks   ☐ Hair Loss

☐ Brain Fog   ☐ Depression

☐ Skin Rashes   ☐ Food Intolerances

☐ Heart Palpitations   ☐ Insomnia

☐ Frequent Urination   ☐ Weight Gain/Loss

☐ Night Sweats   ☐ Silent Reflux

☐ Sensitivity to Sound   ☐ Joint Pain

☐ Difficulty Swallowing   ☐ GI Issues

☐ Low Libido   ☐ Candida

☐ Muscle Weakness   ☐ Migraines

☐ Sensitivity to Light   ☐ Dry Eyes

☐ Dehydration

☐ Intolerance to Heat or Cold

☐ Leaky Gut, IBS or SIBO

☐ Recurrent Infections

☐ Pain/Burning around Implants

☐ Hypo/Hyper Thyroid Symptoms

☐ Hypo/Hyper Adrenal Symptoms

☐ Symptoms of Fibromyalgia

☐ Symptoms of Lyme Disease

☐ Symptoms of EBV

☐ Mast Cell Activation Syndrome

☐ Feeling Like You Are Dying

☐ Symptoms/Diagnosis of Auto-Immune disease

      ☐ Other _____

      ☐ Other _____

      ☐ Other _____

_____

_____

_____

Symptoms list from www.healingbreastimplantillness.com

♥ Journal Your Journey ♥

2 years post op

_____

_____

_____

_____

_____

_____

_____

_____

_____

_____

_____

_____

_____

_____

_____

_____

_____

_____

Symptoms~2 years

After two years post explant, are there any leftover symptoms you are experiencing? Don't forget to look back and see how far you have come from the beginning of your journey!

☐ Chronic Fatigue   ☐ Fever

☐ Ear Ringing   ☐ Acne

☐ Swollen Lymph Nodes   ☐ Vision Issues

☐ Anxiety/Panic Attacks   ☐ Hair Loss

☐ Brain Fog   ☐ Depression

☐ Skin Rashes   ☐ Food Intolerances

☐ Heart Palpitations   ☐ Insomnia

☐ Frequent Urination   ☐ Weight Gain/Loss

☐ Night Sweats   ☐ Silent Reflux

☐ Sensitivity to Sound   ☐ Joint Pain

☐ Difficulty Swallowing   ☐ GI Issues

☐ Low Libido   ☐ Candida

☐ Muscle Weakness   ☐ Migraines

☐ Sensitivity to Light   ☐ Dry Eyes

- ☐ Dehydration
- ☐ Intolerance to Heat or Cold
- ☐ Leaky Gut, IBS or SIBO
- ☐ Recurrent Infections
- ☐ Pain/Burning around Implants
- ☐ Hypo/Hyper Thyroid Symptoms
- ☐ Hypo/Hyper Adrenal Symptoms
- ☐ Symptoms of Fibromyalgia
- ☐ Symptoms of Lyme Disease
- ☐ Symptoms of EBV
- ☐ Mast Cell Activation Syndrome
- ☐ Feeling Like You Are Dying
- ☐ Symptoms/Diagnosis of Auto-Immune disease
    - ☐ Other _____
    - ☐ Other _____
    - ☐ Other _____

_____

_____

_____

~Flare-ups~

Our healing comes in waves. We all have difficult times in our healing journey. Flare ups are a reality for survivors of Breast Implant Illness. We must remember that our heal will never look identical to another's. Use this space to come back and document your flare ups so you can keep track of them.

~ Do they come at a certain time?

~ Are they triggered by something specific?

~ How long do they last?

~ What helps you get through them?

_____

_____

_____

_____

_____

_____

_____

"Just because you are struggling,
doesn't mean you are failing"

_____
_____
_____
_____
_____
_____
_____
_____
_____
_____
_____
_____
_____
_____
_____
_____
_____
_____
_____

"Strength comes from the struggle"

_____

_____

_____

_____

_____

_____

_____

_____

_____

_____

_____

_____

_____

_____

_____

_____

_____

_____

_____

_____

_____

~I am not telling you it's going to be easy,
but it will be worth it ~

_____
_____
_____
_____
_____
_____
_____
_____
_____
_____
_____
_____
_____
_____
_____
_____
_____
_____
_____
_____
_____

H.O.P.E.
~Hold On Pain Ends~

_____

_____

_____

_____

_____

_____

_____

_____

_____

_____

_____

_____

_____

_____

_____

_____

_____

_____

Let it hurt. Let it heal. Let it go.

_____

_____

_____

_____

_____

_____

_____

_____

_____

_____

_____

_____

_____

_____

_____

_____

_____

_____

~Detox~

You are going to collect a lot of info about detoxification after explant. Use this section to make notes on recommendations you get in regards to detox processes that may work best for you. (Keeping in mind that everybody is different, use your best judgement when following detox protocols. It's always best to consult with a trusted medical/holistic professional).

_____

_____

_____

_____

_____

_____

_____

_____

_____

_____

_____

Healing

"True forgiveness is when you can say, thank you for that experience"
~Oprah Winfrey

~The Heal is Real~

How is healing happening for you? Keep in mind there is no right or wrong time frame to heal. You must remember how long you were ill and how sick you were at the time of your explant. These things, as well as our genetics, dietary lifestyle and environment play a role in our healing.

Looking back at your journey, notice how far you've come since discovery of Breast Implant Illness. Some women see huge improvements immediately and others notice small subtle changes, but they are changes nonetheless. We must take notice of these small steps forward and be grateful for our progress. Be kind & gentle with our bodies to encourage the heal to continue.

How is your heal real? Document the changes you notice, both big & small. What are the amazing things about your healing? Your body is miraculous! How has it surprised you along your healing journey?

♥ Journal Your Journey ♥

The Heal is real-ly difficult...

We all have a vison of how our healing journey will go, however, the reality is that healing happens at a different pace for all survivors of Breast Implant Illness. Healing can be hard. It's messy at times and the journey can be a long one.

In our BII community, it can be difficult not to compare your heal to other women. Maybe you were blessed to begin feeling 'the heal' right away. Maybe your healing is more delayed. There is NO RIGHT WAY to heal··· it's only YOUR WAY! Try not to compare!

Use this space to reflect on the more difficult aspects of your healing. You are NOT alone! Every 'body' will heal differently and at different speeds. Just as our illnesses were similar, yet different··· so is our recovery. There is no rule in Breast Implant Illness saying you've failed in some way if your heal looks messier than someone else's.

This is your space, speak your truth, talk about the messy times of your healing and how that has made you feel. Healing is an emotional rollercoaster. Acknowledge and document your ups & downs... it's the only way to move forward.

_____

_____

_____

_____

_____

_____

_____

_____

_____

_____

_____

_____

_____

_____

_____

A moment of silence

There is a moment of time after explant where every woman needs to take time to mourn her loss. The loss of expectations for how things were supposed to go. The loss of your implants or your breasts (for our post mastectomy sisters). The loss of friends or family members and the time you lost while you were so ill.

You must honor these losses in order to move forward in your healing. Honor the anger, resentment or hatred for your loss. Use this space to acknowledge what has been taken from you. This process will help you continue to move on.

_____

_____

_____

_____

_____

_____

_____

~Grateful~

Let's take a moment at this point in your healing to be grateful. What are you feeling most grateful for? If you are having a hard time finding gratitude, try to think back to when you first discovered Breast Implant Illness. How far have you come since then?

"Gratitude turns what we have into enough"
~Anonymous~

_____

_____

_____

_____

_____

_____

_____

_____

~Self-love~

Self-love is NOT self-ish! Love is the greatest gift you can bestow upon yourself. You are not greedy for putting yourself first in this life.

The journey of Breast Implant Illness gave me such a greater appreciation for my body and all that it is and does for me.

Think about how hard your body has been working for you. Through the years you were sick, surviving explant surgery and this journey of healing, your body has fought like a warrior.

On the next few pages, take time to love & appreciate your body for all that it's done up until now and all that it will continue to do for you as you find your highest level of healing.

**"Owning our story
and loving ourselves through that process,
is the bravest thing that we'll ever do."
~Brene Brown~**

♥ Journal Your Journey ♥

Write an apology letter to your body, for all it has been through.

Dear Body,

I am sorry for...

_____

_____

_____

_____

_____

_____

_____

_____

_____

_____

_____

_____

_____

_____

_____

_____

_____

Now take a moment to write a Thank you note to your body. Thank her for all she does for you. Regardless if your implants were for enhancement or reconstruction, your body deserves praise for how hard she works.

~ We are all warriors ~

Dear Body,

Thank you for...

_____

_____

_____

_____

_____

_____

_____

_____

_____

_____

_____

_____

Everyone needs a pep-talk now and then. On the next few lines, tell your body what you'd like to accomplish together in your healing journey. Remind her how strong she is and that "she's got this". Visualize what your full healing looks like and write it down.

_____

_____

_____

_____

_____

_____

_____

_____

_____

_____

_____

_____

_____

_____

Let's take a moment to love on yourself now. Maybe you are thrilled with your results, maybe you are left feeling sad about what's left of your chest, maybe you are completely flat due to previous breast cancer. No matter what our situation, we should value and cherish our bodies for all that they are and all that they can do. Use this space to remind yourself about all the ways your body is amazing!

_____
_____
_____
_____
_____
_____
_____
_____
_____
_____
_____
_____
_____

We must remember that there is no body part which defines you. You are beautiful for so many reasons and none of them have to do with your breasts.

Take a moment to acknowledge what defines you?

_____

_____

_____

_____

_____

_____

_____

_____

_____

_____

_____

_____

_____

_____

_____

_____

~Blessings~

Many women find that this journey of Breast Implant Illness is full of blessings along the way. A huge part of healing is finding the rainbow in the storm.

What have been some blessings that you have experienced along the way?

> "The thankful heart opens our eyes
> to a multitude of blessings
> that continually surround us."
> ~James E. Faust

_____

_____

_____

_____

_____

_____

_____

~Thankful~

So many things to be thankful for in our journey. Health, happiness, renewed faith. Thankful we discovered Breast Implant Illness. Thankful we explanted. Thankful for the friends/family who have supported us along our way. Thankful for our surgeon. Thankful for the sisterhood that surrounds us in this community.

What are you most thankful for?

_____

_____

_____

_____

_____

_____

_____

_____

_____

_____

~Dear Old Me~

If you could go back in time, back to whatever situation that led you to choose implants, what would you say to your old self? How would you warn her? Would she have listened? Could you tell her she was beautiful just the way she was? Would you let her know that regardless if she wanted an augmentation or required reconstruction, those implants were not going to 'complete her' or make her 'whole' or 'normal'?

Dear Old Me...

_____

_____

_____

_____

_____

_____

_____

_____

#notourdaughters

We must teach our girls to value themselves for who they are and what gifts they bring to others, not for how they look. Boys need to learn the pressures that women feel this day in age. We must teach our boys to look beyond the physical beauty of a woman and cherish her soul, rather than certain body parts.

We have all taken away valuable lessons from this experience of Breast Implant Illness. There are things we have learned along the way that would be a priceless gift to pass down. Regardless if you have daughters or sons, maybe you do not yet have children, you certainly know some children··· what would you want them to know?

Dear Children~

_____

_____

_____

_____

~Changes~

One thing is for sure, we are never the same after Breast Implant Illness. For many, this illness is our lowest point, our darkest hour. It's hard not to be changed by that in some way. How are you different since surviving Breast Implant Illness?

**"Never to suffer,
would never to have been blessed"
~Edgar Allen Poe~**

_____

_____

_____

_____

_____

_____

_____

_____

_____

Let Me Get This OFF My CHEST

It's time now, for you, to get this off your chest.
Document your story...

from illness to healing.

_____

_____

_____

_____

_____

_____

_____

_____

_____

_____

_____

_____

_____

_____

_____

_____

Dear Sisters,

Healing from Breast Implant Illness is more of an emotional process than any of us initially realize. I pray that taking the time to document your journey has helped you heal in some way. Breast Implant Illness is one of those experiences that tends to knock the wind out of you. Finding the time to process the experience is allowing yourself to honor all the feelings and emotions that come with this illness. If we don't take the time to acknowledge what has happened, we may find ourselves never fully healing.

I created this journal so that my BII sisters would know that we must honor the emotions to fully process the experience. Then we take time to recognize the strong warriors we are, let go of the hurt and anger and move forward.

We are all pieces of the same story! Many of us are left with some physical reminders of our illness. We should all have the opportunity to fully heal emotionally from Breast Implant Illness in order to allow our highest level of health.

Live well, my warrior sisters, live well.

♥Tara

Made in the USA
Columbia, SC
08 August 2021

43217223R00081